Write your name:

Cc Kk

Some Spanish dancers are performing. The ladies wear bright dresses and click castanets, *ck*, *ck*, *ck, ck*.

Action: Snap your fingers together in the air as if you are playing castanets, and say *c, k, ck, ck*.

The letters ‹c› and ‹k› make the same sound. To help remember the different shapes, we call them:

E e

Snake is very fond of eggs. He cracks them open, *e, e, e, egg.* Inky and Bee prefer chocolate eggs!

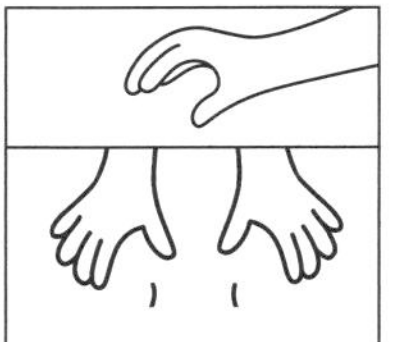

Action: Pretend to crack an egg against the side of a pan with one hand. Use both hands to open the shell, saying *e, e, e, e*.

Help hen get to her eggs. Keep inside the lines.

e

egg

nest

ten

pen

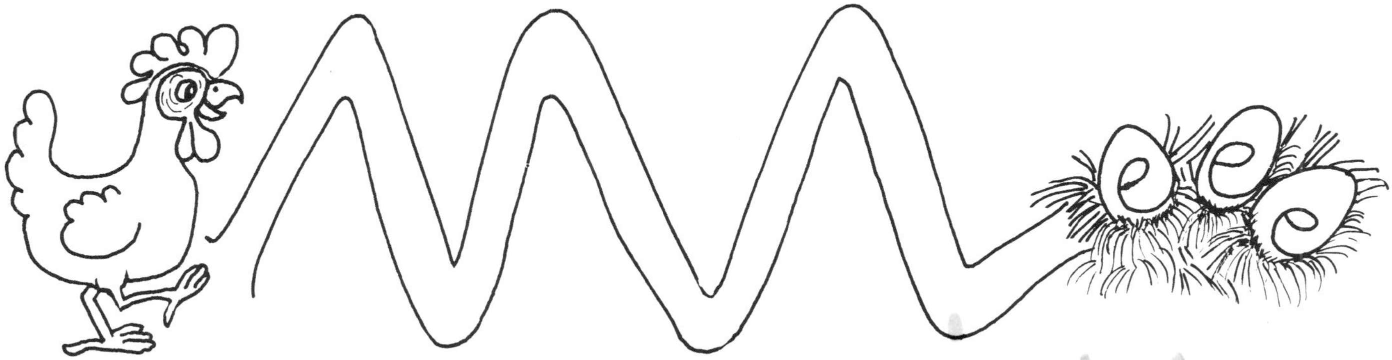

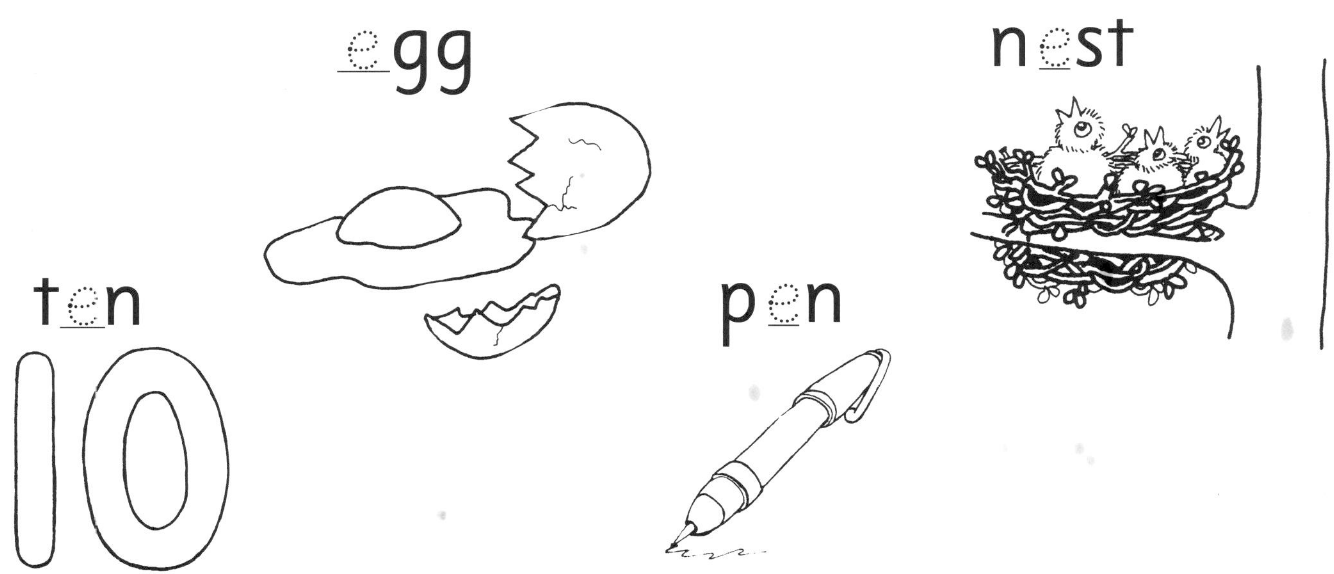

H h

Inky and Bee are having a hopping race. When they finish they are hot and tired, huffing *h*, *h*, *h.*

Action: Hold your hand up to your mouth as if you are out of breath, and say *h, h, h, h*.

Help frog hop to his lily pad. Keep inside the lines.

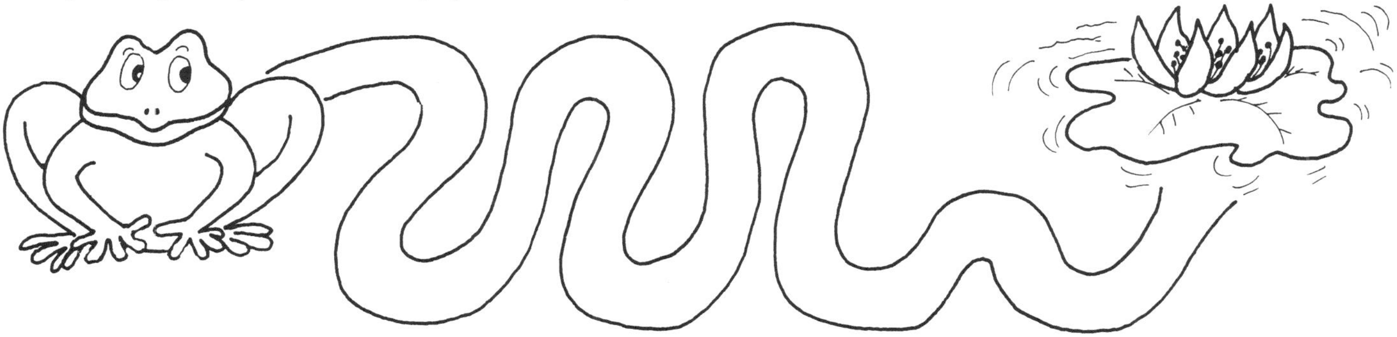

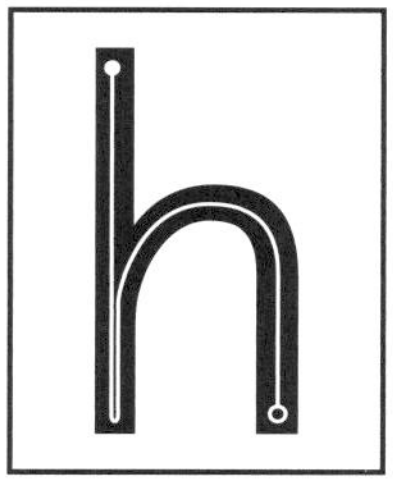

h h h h h h h

h h h h h h h h

hiss

hand

hen

hat

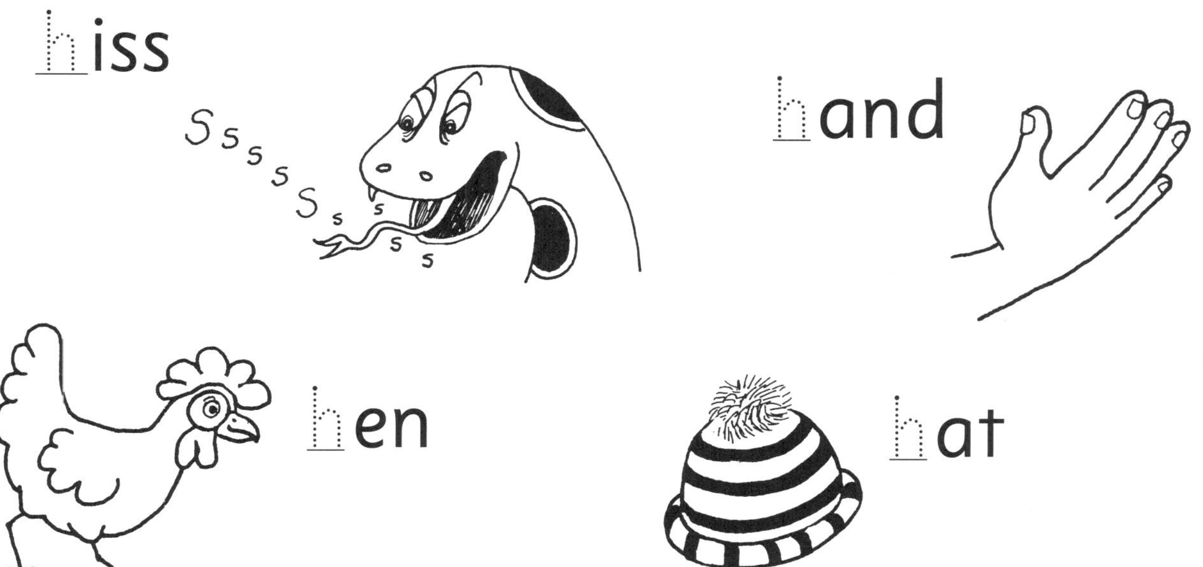

R r

The puppy has a special piece of rag. He holds on to it and pulls, shaking his head and growling *rrrrrr*.

Action: Pretend to be a puppy pulling a rag and shake your head from side to side, saying *rrrrrr*.

Help the rabbit run to his burrow. Keep inside the lines.

r

r r r r r r r r

r r r r r r r

rip

rat

racket

cricket

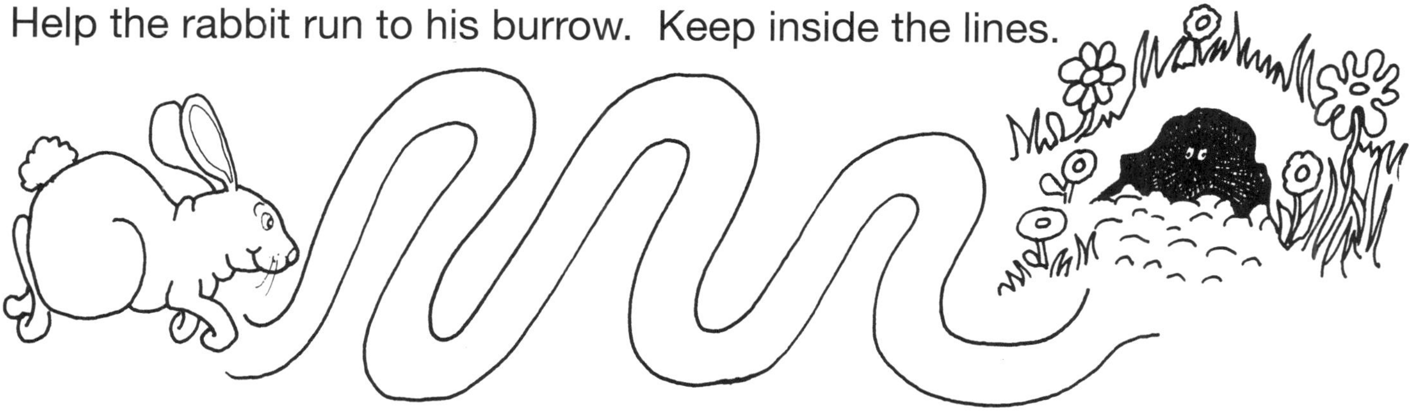

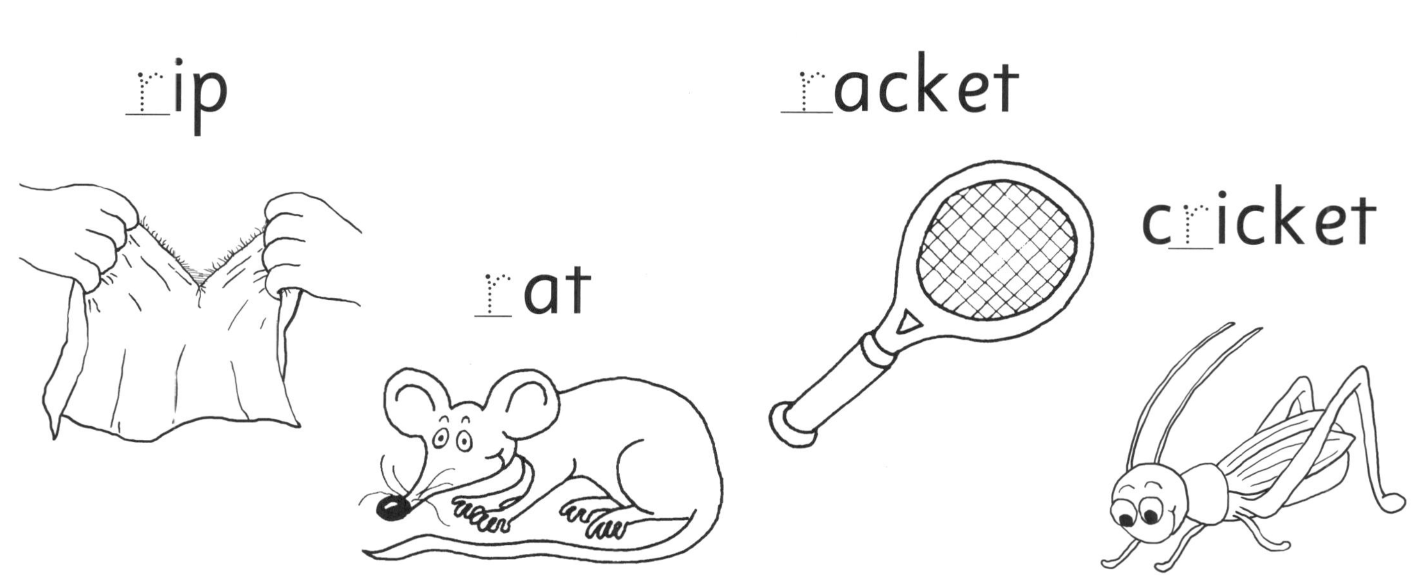

Snake likes to eat eggs best of all. Inky prefers cheese and Bee likes honey. When they see their food they rub their tummies and say *mmmmmm.*

Action: Rub your tummy as if you can see some tasty food, and say *mmmmmm*.

Help mole get back to his molehill. Keep inside the lines.

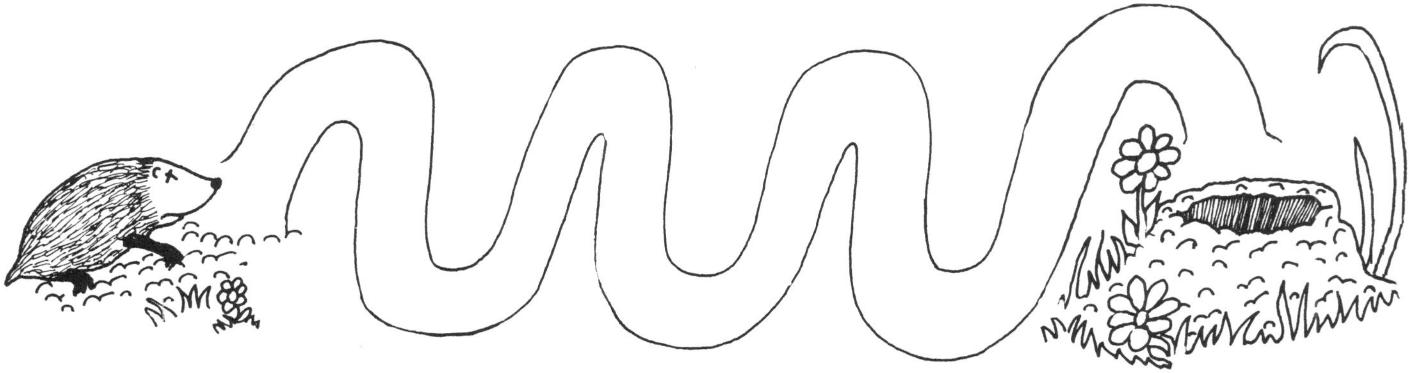

m

m m m m m

m m m m m

map

stamp

mat

man

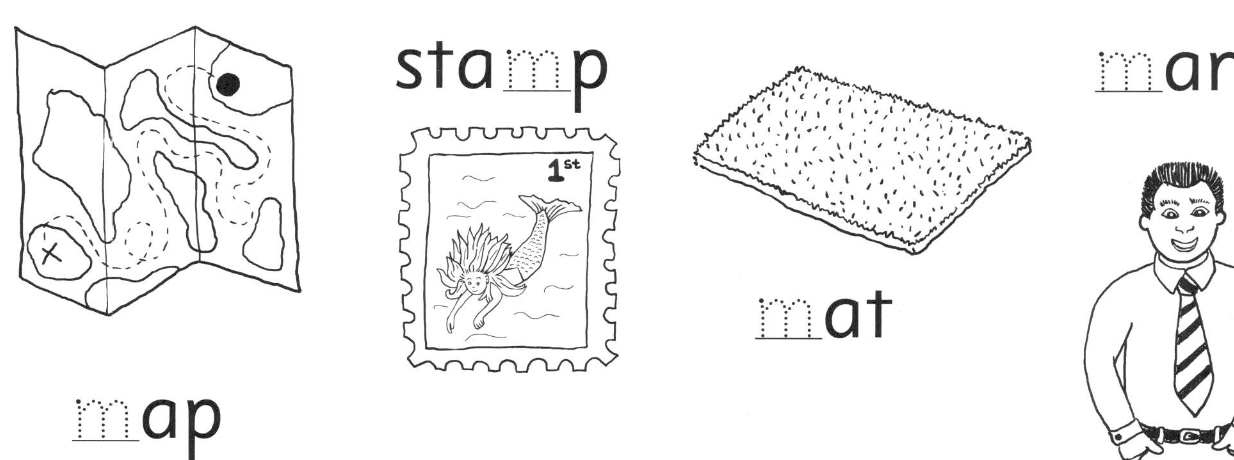

Inky, Snake, and Bee have found an old toy drum. They all have a go at banging the drum, *d, d, d, d*.

D d

Action: Move your hands up and down as if you are beating a drum, and say *d, d, d, d*.

Take the dog back to his kennel. Keep inside the lines.

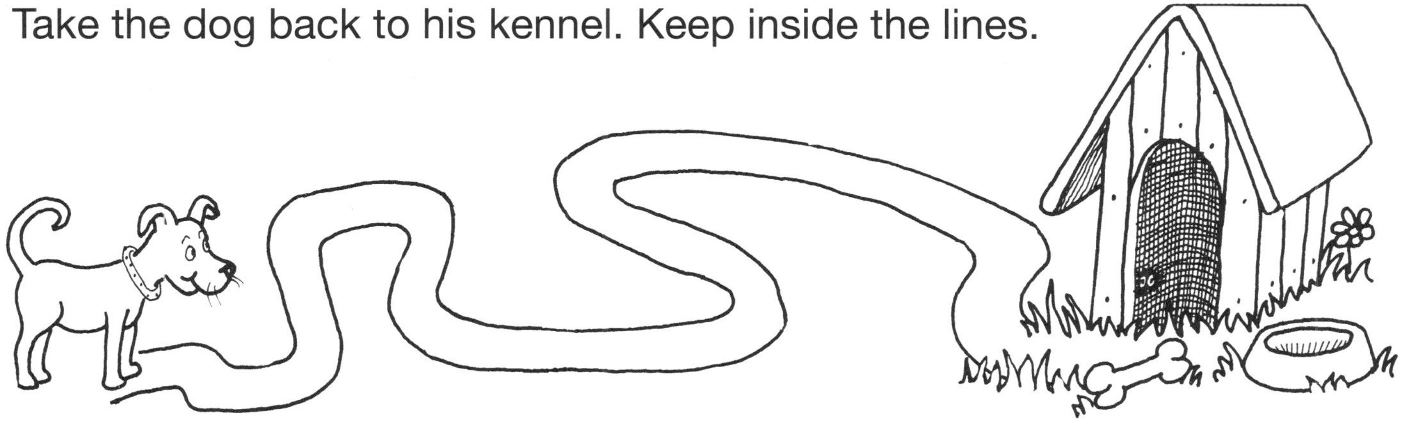

d

d d d d d

d d d d d d d d

dress

hand

drink

desk

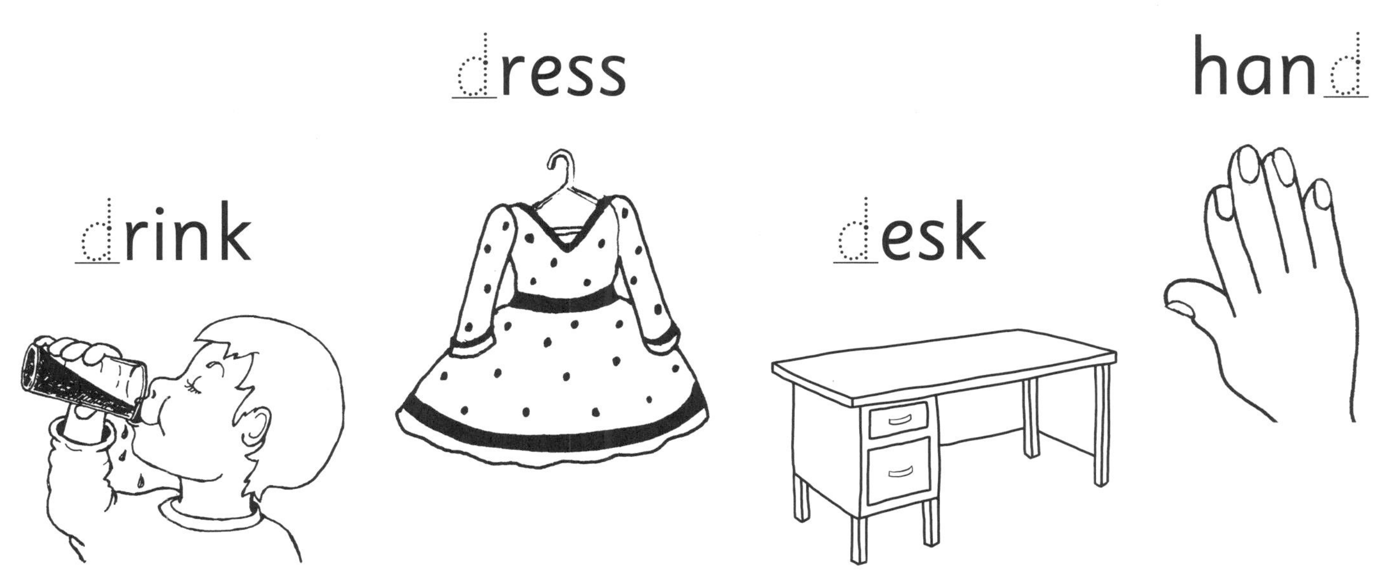

Join each picture to the letter for the sound it begins with.

Practice the ‹c› shape.

Caterpillar /c/

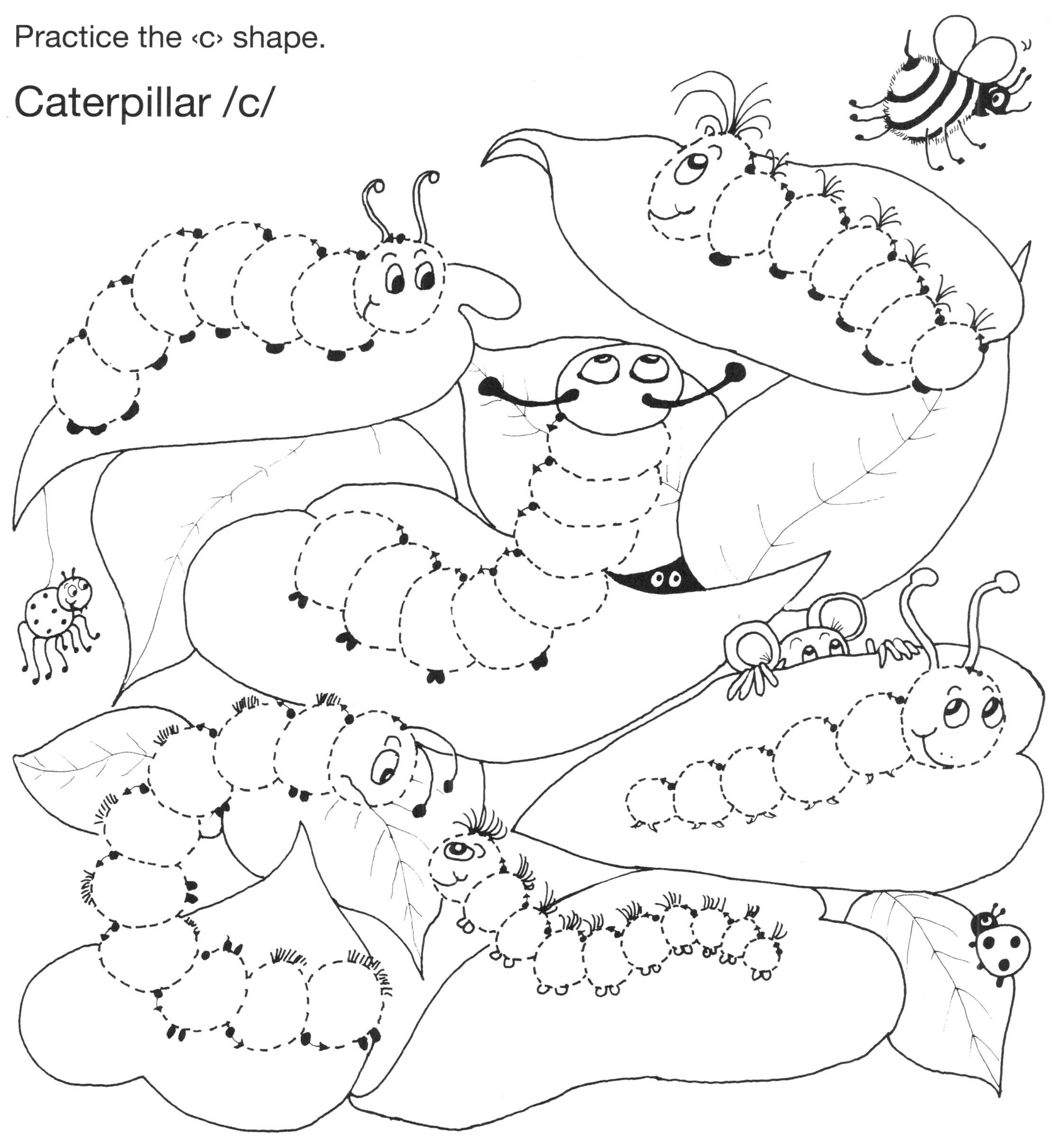

Write the letter for the sound at the end of each word.

How to make this book:

1. Cut along the dotted lines.
2. Put the top sheet on top of the other. Fold in half.

Note: This book is intended for use when the children have completed this workbook, including reading double sounds (/ck/, /tt/ etc.).

②

Rats!

⑦

Red hen pecks at a sack.

A cat and a kitten.

⑤

Red hen sits and rests.

Red Hen

1

Red hen has hidden in a sack.
Kitten pats it.

6

Red hen sits on a nest.

When two letters that make the same sound come together, as with ‹c› and ‹k›, you only say the sound once. Trace over the letters, read the word, and draw a picture.

Write in the missing letters. Then read the word and draw a picture in the space.

Trace over the dotted lines.

Can you hear the sound in the words? In each row, cross out the picture of the word without that sound.

1 2

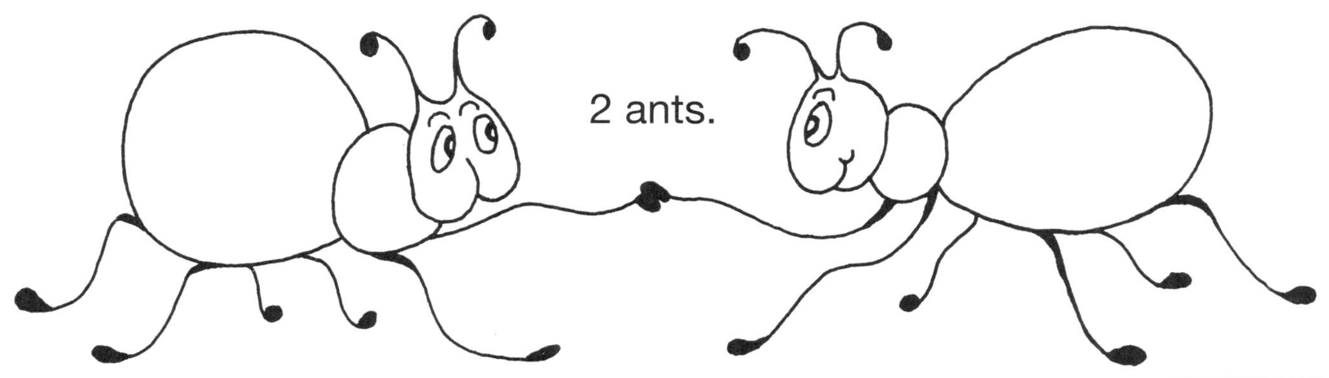

Trace over the dotted lines to write the number 2.

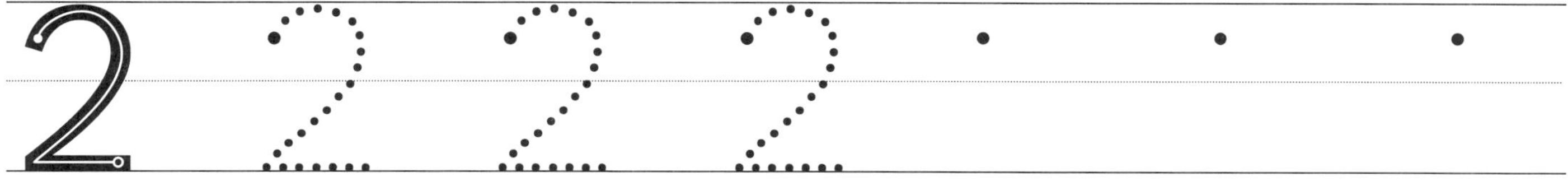

Find the 2 ants.

Eggs-panding hair!

Stand half an egg shell in a pot and give it a face. Put in some damp cotton balls or paper. Sprinkle some cress or other small seeds onto it. Wait for a few days and watch the "hair" grow!

Mmmm meal

Stick pictures of tasty food onto a paper plate.

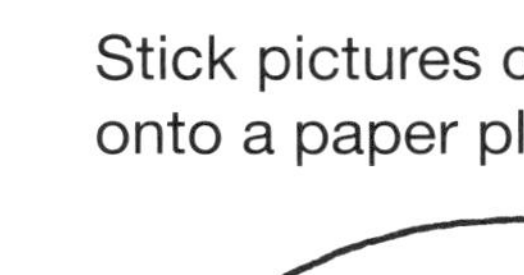

Edible letters

Make the mixture for some plain cookies or biscuits. Cut out letter shapes from a piece of card. Put the letter shapes onto the rolled-out mix and cut around them.

Name card

Get an adult to write your name for you. Cut out a piece of card, about 4" x 8". Copy your name onto the card.